GW00359352

Crossword Poems

Volume Two

Crossword Poems

An Anthology of a different kind

Volume Two

ₚ

PARSIMONY PRESS
2000

There are a number of living people who made it
possible to bring these books into print. But the real
dedication should be to the people whose verse is
included, and to those whose verse should have been
included had there been room to do so.

First published in the UK in 2000
Second impression 2000
by Parsimony Press Ltd
West Huntspill, Somerset

Introduction and selection copyright
© Robert Norton, 2000.

ISBN 1 902979 11 7

Typesetting by MacDonald, Miles & Russell Enterprises
Printed and bound by Tien Wah Press, Singapore

It was around the 1950s when schools stopped teaching many of the things that had been part of what every child was exposed to for a great many years. Latin slipped off the curriculum. If there was poetry in the new lessons it tended to become contemporary poetry, much of which lacked the strict rhyme and meter that made learning stuff slightly less of a pain.

In those days the cryptic crosswords that appeared in papers like *The Times* were loaded with allusions that it was expected everybody would recognise. 'Let the dog see the rabbit' was the compiler's motto, and it was rare not to have a quotation with a missing word which gave the solver a start. The number of people who could quote more than four lines of Byron's poem *The Destruction of Sennacherib* would probably have fitted easily into a telephone box. But the number of people who knew the lines *'The Assyrian came down like the wolf on the fold, And his cohorts were gleaming in purple and gold'* might have, with ease, filled all the football stadiums in Britain and still have many to spare.

These books are to remind those who were born before the Hitler War of what they once knew, and to introduce those born after to what their parents and grandparents once knew. The lines in red are those the crossword clues could have drawn from. The rest is what the compilers reasonably assumed had been forgotten. Every now and then there is a loose word in black. That is because when people have been asked to repeat what they remember they have commonly got one word wrong.

As in volume one, the poems are given to you in alphabetical order, like an index of first lines.

*Shelley had much more of a life before he was drowned at
the age of 30 than can be even hinted at in a paragraph or
two. It really is worth reading about him, even if only in
a Biographical Dictionary. Most of us know him only as
a poet with a rather complicated love life. But his prose
writing, his essays, his political writing, and perhaps
above all his mischievousness seem to have been lost in our
understanding of him.*

And like a dying lady lean and pale
Who totters forth, wrapp'd in a gauzy veil,
Out of her chamber, led by the insane
And feeble wanderings of her fading brain,
The moon arose up in the murky east
A white and shapeless mass.

Art thou pale for weariness
Of climbing heaven and gazing on the earth,
   Wandering companionless
Among the stars that have a different birth,
And ever changing, like a joyless eye
That finds no object worth its constancy?

Sir Thomas Wyatt was born of a Yorkshire family in 1503, and lasted another thirty-nine years. It is surprising that in a busy and dangerous life he managed to write as much poetry as he did. It is also surprising that it is so little known today, especially since much of it pre-dates Donne, Marlowe and others in pleading with wit and charm for the affections of various ladies. It is even more surprising that he survived as long 39 years, since it appears that his pleadings were often successful.

He was always taking diplomatic posts for Henry the Eighth, and was an admirer of Catherine of Aragon. Perhaps because he admitted to Henry the Eighth that he had been a lover of Ann Boleyn and therefore was in a position to say that she was not a suitable queen that he was not executed as were her other lovers. After a spell in prison, in which he wrote complaining verses less kindly than Raleigh's were in later years, he was sent as ambassador to the court Charles V in France. This period of forgiveness slightly suffered after the execution of his friend and protector Thomas Cromwell in 1540. But he was still given tasks by the king, and it was of a fever contracted on his last one that he died, fulfilling the mournful predictions in many of his poems.

> And wilt thou leave me thus?
>   Say nay, say nay, for shame!
> —To save thee from the blame
> Of all my grief and grame.
> And wilt thou leave me thus?
>   Say nay! Say nay!

And wilt thou leave me thus?
That hath loved thee so long
In wealth and woe among:
And is thy heart so strong
As for to leave me thus?
   Say nay! Say nay!

And wilt thou leave me thus,
That hath given thee my heart
Never for to depart
Neither for pain nor smart:
And wilt thou leave me thus?
   Say nay! Say nay!

And wilt thou leave me thus,
And have no more pitye
Of him that loveth thee?
Alas, thy cruelty!
And wilt thou leave me thus?
   Say nay! Say nay!

BLOW, BLOW, THOU WINTER WIND
WILLIAM SHAKESPEARE (1564-1616)

There isn't anything to add to what has already been written about Shakespeare. Many of the speeches in his plays are known by everyone. 'To be or not to be' 'Friends, Romans and countrymen, lend me your ears' and so on. Many are also misquoted, like 'Lay on, Mac-Duff' as an invitation to start the fight, has become 'Lead on, MacDuff'. But the songs in his plays are memorable even before they have been set to music.

Blow, blow, thou winter wind,
   Thou art not so unkind
     As man's ingratitude;
   Thy tooth is not so keen,
   Because thou art not seen,
     Although thy breath be rude.
Heigh ho! sing, heigh ho! unto the green holly:
Most friendship is feigning, most loving mere folly:
     Then heigh ho, the holly!
     This life is most jolly.

   Freeze, freeze, thou bitter sky,
   That dost not bite so nigh
     As benefits forgot:
   Though thou the waters warp,
   Thy sting is not so sharp,
     As friend remember'd not.
Heigh ho! sing, heigh ho! unto the green holly:
Most friendship is feigning, most loving mere folly:
     Then heigh ho, the holly!
     This life is most jolly.

This bit from The Lay of the Last Minstrel *is an example of the epic poem that launched Walter Scott's literary career. It was 1805, and he was thirty-four years old and had been a barrister for 13 years and sheriff depute of Selkirkshire for six. What he had written to precede it had reflected his interest in French and German poetry and in Scottish Border history, but these were the writings of an amateur who earned his living in other ways. Perhaps the success of* The Lay *pointed him in other directions. He joined John Ballantyne in his printing works, he wrote for* The Edinburgh Review, *and helped to found* The Quarterly Review. *And with Ballantyne they started bookselling. This was a seriously busy man, and for much of his life he still found time to commute on horseback forty miles each way at least once a week to honour one of his obligations.*

Unlike his earlier books which were published anonymously, he published his verse in his own name, and it became popular enough for him to be offered the Laureateship in 1813. At his suggestion it went to Southey instead, Southey being the poet most derided, with some justification, by his contemporaries. Nevertheless, despite this, Southey's worth learning more about if only because he gave us 'Curses are like young chickens, they always come home to roost.'

But, you ask, what about Scott? His books. Ah, yes.

It was in 1814 that a book called Waverley *appeared anonymously. Scott by then was forty three years old, and people were busy with a Corsican called Napoleon Bonaparte. It was no time to rock his boat, since nobody*

11

knew how the book would be received. After that book followed book, sometimes more than one a year. Ivanhoe was published in 1819, and the following year Scott was knighted, still only a respectable landowner, printer, publisher and poet. In 1826 Ballantyne's of which he was still a partner, became involved in the bankruptcy of Constables, and they were landed with a debt of £114,000. If this is not chicken feed today, in those days it was a really serious amount of money. Twenty-five years later the whole Crystal Palace was built for not much more.

Scott took on the debt himself.

It was not until 1827, when he was nearly sixty that he admitted to the novels. And it was soon after his death in 1832 that   their continuing success allowed the outstanding remainder to be paid in full.

It is tempting to write more about this man, since he is perceived as so different to the man he really was. But we must content ourselves with pointing you at J G Lockhart's life, which was published only five years after his death, and which is considered one of the great biographies in the English language.

Breathes there the man, with soul so dead,
Who never to himself hath said,
This is my own, my native land!
Whose heart hath ne'er within him burned,
As home his footsteps he hath turned,
From wandering on a foreign strand!
If such there breathe, go, mark him well;
For him no Minstrel raptures swell;
High though his titles, proud his name,
Boundless his wealth as wish can claim;

Despite those titles, power, and pelf,
The wretch, concentred all in self,
Living, shall forfeit, fair renown,
And doubly dying, shall go down
To the vile dust, from whence he sprung,
Unwept, unhonoured, and unsung.

O Caledonia! Stern and wild,
Meet nurse for a poetic child!
Land of brown heath and shaggy wood,
Land of the mountain and the flood,
Land of my sires! What mortal hand
Can e'er untie the filial band,
That knits me to thy rugged strand!
Still as I view each well-known scene,
Think what is now, and what hath been,
Seems as, to me, of all bereft,
Sole friends thy woods and streams were left;
And thus I love them better still,
Even in extremity of ill.
By Yarrow's stream still let me stray,
Though none should guide my feeble way;
Still feel the breeze down Ettrick break,
Although it chill my withered cheek;
Still lay my head by Teviot Stone,
Though there, forgotten and alone,
The Bard my draw his parting groan.

It is The Charge of the Light Brigade *that most people know. There is, in fact, even a very early recording of him reading it. But* Maud *and* The Lady of Shallot *run it a close second. One day, when you have a bit more time, have a go at* Morte d'Arthur, *which has done as much as anything to preserve the legend of a king who was probably little like what he has been cracked up to be.*

Come into the garden, Maud,
   For the black bat, Night, has flown,
Come into the garden, Maud,
   I am here at the gate alone;
And the woodbine spices are wafted abroad,
   And the musk of the roses blown.

For a breeze of morning moves,
   And the planet of Love is on high,
Beginning to faint in the light that she loves
   On a bed of daffodil sky,
To faint in the light of the sun she loves,
   To faint in his light, and to die.

All night have the roses heard
   The flute, violin, bassoon;
All night has the casement jessamine stirr'd
   To the dancers dancing in tune;
Till a silence fell with the waking bird,
   And a hush with the setting moon.

I said to the lily, 'There is but one
    With whom she has heart to be gay.
When will the dancers leave her alone?
    She is weary of dance and play.'
Now half to the setting moon are gone,
    And half to the rising day;
Low on the sand and loud on the stone
    The last wheel echoes away.

I said to the rose, 'The brief night goes
    In babble and revel and wine.
O young lord-lover, what sighs are those
    For one that will never be thine?
But mine, but mine,' so I swear to the rose
    'For ever and ever, mine.'

And the soul of the rose went into my blood,
    As the music clash'd in the hall;
And long by the garden lake I stood,
    For I heard your rivulet fall
From the lake to the meadow and on to the wood,
    Our wood, that is dearer than all;

From the meadow your walks have left so sweet
    That whenever a March-wind sighs
He sets the jewel-print of your feet
    In violets blue as your eyes,
To the woody hollows in which we meet
    And the valleys of paradise.

The slender acacia would not shake
    One long milk-bloom on the tree;
The white lake-blossom fell into the lake,

As the pimpernel dozed on the lea;
But the rose was awake all night for your sake,
    Knowing your promise to me;
The lilies and roses were all awake,
    They sigh'd for the dawn and thee.

Queen rose of the rosebud garden of girls,
Come hither, the dances are done,
In gloss of satin and glimmer of pearls,
Queen lily and rose in one;
Shine out, little head, sunning over with curls,
    To the flowers, and be their sun.

There has fallen a splendid tear
    From the passion-flower at the gate.
She is coming, my dove, my dear;
    She is coming, my life, my fate;
The red rose cries, 'She is near, she is near;'
    And the white rose weeps, 'She is late;'
The larkspur listens, 'I hear, I hear;'
    And the lily whispers, 'I wait.'

She is coming, my own, my sweet;
    Were it ever so airy a tread,
My heart would hear her and beat,
    Were it earth in an earthy bed;
My dust would hear her and beat,
    Had I lain for a century dead;
Would start and tremble under her feet,
    And blossom in purple and red.

Marlowe is chiefly remembered for his plays, for his rivalry with Shakespeare, whose historical plays were much influenced by him, for the trouble he was always in with the law in both England and Holland, and for ending up being killed in a tavern after a quarrel over a bill. This was by no means the first fight he had been in. People like this, like Mercutio in Romeo and Juliet, are always appealing. But it seems to be accepted that Mercutio was not modelled on Marlowe, but rather that the dead shepherd in As You Like It *was.*

Come live with me and be my Love,
And we will all the pleasures prove
That hills and valleys, dales and fields,
Or woods or steepy mountain yields.

And we will sit upon the rocks,
And see the shepherds feed their flocks
By shallow rivers, to whose falls
Melodious birds sing madrigals.

And I will make thee beds of roses
And a thousand fragrant posies;
A cap of flowers, and a kirtle
Embroider'd all with leaves of myrtle.

A gown made of the finest wool
Which from our pretty lambs we pull;
Fair-linèd slippers for the cold,
With buckles of the purest gold.

A belt of straw and ivy-buds
With coral clasps and amber studs:
And if these pleasures may thee move,
Come live with me and be my Love.

The shepherd swains shall dance and sing
For thy delight each May morning:
If these delights thy mind may move,
Then live with me and be my Love.

Come unto these yellow sands,
    And then take hands:
Court'sied when you have, and kiss'd,—
    The wild waves whist,—
Foot it featly here and there;
And, sweet sprites, the burthen bear.
        Hark, hark!
            Bow, wow,
        The watch-dogs bark:
            Bow, wow.
        Hark, hark! I hear
The strain of strutting chanticleer
Cry, Cock-a-diddle-dow!

UPON WESTMINSTER BRIDGE
WILLIAM WORDSWORTH

*The funny thing about this famous sonnet is that so many
years later, with all the building and rebuilding that has
taken place since Wordsworth wrote it, it is still possible to
get up early on a summer morning, before the traffic has
got heavy, and see exactly what he saw, or at least feel
exactly what he felt.*

Earth has not anything to show more fair:
Dull would he be of soul who could pass by
   A sight so touching in its majesty:
This City now doth like a garment wear
The beauty of the morning; silent, bare,
   Ships, towers, domes, theatres, and temples lie
   Open unto the fields, and to the sky;
All bright and glittering in the smokeless air.
Never did sun more beautifully steep
   In his first splendour valley, rock, or hill;
Ne'er saw I, never felt, a calm so deep!
   The river glideth at his own sweet will:
Dear God! the very houses seem asleep;
   And all that mighty heart is lying still!

Full fathom five thy father lies;
Of his bones are coral made;
Those are pearls that were his eyes:
    Nothing of him that doth fade,
But doth suffer a sea-change
Into something rich and strange.
Sea-nymphs hourly ring his knell:
   Ding-dong.
Hark! now I hear them—
   Ding-dong, bell!

As with many people in 16th and 17th centuries, Raleigh's life was not a bed of roses. After the death of Queen Elizabeth he was imprisoned in the tower with his family. After thirteen years he was spared an execution and let out to show people the gold mine he said he found in Guiana in 1596. The trip was a disaster, and he was finally executed in 1618.

This is the poem that he was meant to have written on the eve of his execution. But it seems there are some prodnoses who not only say it wasn't written then, but that it was not even written by him. In many anthologies the poem stops at the line 'But after this, it will thirst no more', *and yet the later half, although it sometimes descends into doggerel, is the more moving and convincing because of that.*
Where there is doubt, go for the best choice. There is enough beautiful writing about mortality in his own handwriting to justify allowing him this last glorious poem.

Give me my scallop-shell of quiet,
  My staff of faith to walk upon,
My scrip of joy, immortal diet,
  My bottle of salvation,
My gown of glory, hope's true gage
And thus I'll take my pilgrimage.

Blood must be my body's balmer
  No other balm will there be given,
Whilst my soul, like a white palmer,
  Travels to the land of heaven;
Over the silver mountains,

Where spring the nectar fountains:
    There I will kiss
    The bowl of bliss;
And drink mine everlasting fill
On every milken hill.
My soul will be a-dry before;
But, after, it will thirst no more.

Then by that happy blissful day,
More peaceful pilgrims I shall see,
That have cast off their rags of clay
And walk apparelled fresh like me.
    I'll take them first
    To quench their thirst
And taste of nectar suckets,
    At those clear wells
    Where sweetness dwells,
Drawn up by saints in crystal buckets.

And when our bottles and all we
Are filled with immortality,
Then the blessèd paths we'll travel,
Strowed with rubies thick as gravel;
    Ceilings of diamonds, sapphire floors,
High walls of coral and pearly bowers.
From thence to heaven's bribeless hall,
Where no corrupted voices brawl;
No conscience molten into gold,
    No forged accuser bought or sold,
No cause deferred, no vain-spent journey,
For there Christ is the King's Attorney,
Who pleads for all without degrees,
And He hath angels, but no fees.

And when the grand twelve-million jury
Of our sins, with direful fury,
Against our souls black verdicts give,
Christ pleads His death, and then we live.

Be Thou my speaker, taintless pleader,
Unblotted lawyer, true proceeder!
Thou givest salvation even for alms;
Not with a bribèd lawyer's palms.
And this is mine eternal plea
To Him that made heaven, earth, and sea,
That, since my flesh must die so soon,
And want a head to dine next noon,
Just at the stroke, when my veins start and spread,
Set on my soul an everlasting head!
Then am I ready, like a palmer fit,
To tread those blest paths which before I writ.

*Everybody wrote poems to try to persuade the girls to do
what their mothers had told them not to do. This is one of
the best ever written, and deserves success. We will
probably never know whether it worked. Funnily
enough, although he became well-known in his lifetime,
close to Cromwell, tutoring, spying in Holland (everybody seems to have a go at spying in Holland), satirising
corruption where he found it and being MP for Hull, it
was not really until the twentieth century that people
began to appreciate his poetry. Perhaps you remember
David Niven's line as a bomber pilot in A Matter of Life
and Death* 'Andrew Marvell, what a marvel' *as he
recited these beginning lines.*

> Had we but world enough, and time,
> This coyness, Lady, were no crime
> We would sit down and think which way
> To walk and pass our long love's day.
> Thou by the Indian Ganges' side
> Shouldst rubies find: I by the tide
> Of Humber would **complain**. I would
> Love you ten years before the Flood,
> And you should, if you please, refuse
> Till the conversion of the Jews.
> My vegetable love should grow
> Vaster than empires, and more slow;
> An hundred years should go to praise
> Thine eyes and on thy forehead gaze;
> Two hundred to adore each breast,
> But thirty thousand to the rest;

An age at least to every part,
And the last age should show your heart.
For, Lady, you deserve this state,
Nor would I love at lower rate.
   But at my back I always hear
Time's wingèd chariot hurrying near;
And yonder all before us lie
Deserts of vast eternity.
Thy beauty shall no more be found,
Nor, in thy marble vault, shall sound
My echoing song: then worms shall try
That long preserved virginity,
And your quaint honour turn to dust,
And into ashes all my lust:
The grave's a fine and private place,
But none, I think, do there embrace.
   Now therefore, while the youthful hue
Sits on thy skin like morning dew,
And while thy willing soul transpires
At every pore with instant fires,
Now let us sport us while we may,
And now, like amorous birds of prey,
Rather at once our time devour
Than languish in his slow-chapt power.
Let us roll all our strength and all
Our sweetness up into one ball,
And tear our pleasures with rough strife:
Thorough, the iron gates of life.
Thus, though we cannot make our sun,
Stand still, yet we will make him run.

An American orphan schooled in England, to which he was brought by the tobacco exporter who adopted him, he started life under an assumed name in the US army, perhaps to escape the gambling debts he had run up at the University of Virginia. But he was discharged when he was 22 for neglecting his duties, one of his neglects being the publication of a book of verse which included this poem. His short life was a constant struggle against poverty and alcoholism, and, at the age of forty, he was found dying in a street in Baltimore two years after his young wife died at the age of 24. His output in the second half of his life was nevertheless of greater influence to other writers that almost any of his contemporaries.

Helen, thy beauty is to me
    Like those Nicèan barks of yore
That gently, o'er a perfumed sea,
    The weary way-worn wanderer bore
    To his own native shore.

On desperate seas long wont to roam,
    Thy hyacinth hair, thy classic face,
Thy Naiad airs have brought me home
    To the glory that was Greece,
And the grandeur that was Rome.

Lo, in yon brilliant window-niche
    How statue-like I see thee stand,
The agate lamp within thy hand,
Ah! Psyche, from the regions which
    Are holy land!

Caroline Norton, gloriously, splendidly Irish, was born in 1808. She was the granddaughter of Sheridan the playwright, and was somewhat ahead of her time in temperament and behaviour. Married to an unsuccessful and not entirely agreeable barrister called the Hon. George Norton, she had to take to writing to support herself, him, his drinking, and their three sons. Her first book of verse, The Sorrows of Rosalie, *published in 1829 when she was twenty-one, was an instant success. At the age of twenty-eight she left her husband, who later unsuccessfully sued Lord Melbourne for committing adultery with her.*

Melbourne was at the time Prime Minister for the second time, and it seems improbable that Norton could ever have won the case, even had the protagonists been less appealing on the one hand and more appealing on the other.

Failing in this he also tried through the courts to obtain the income she derived from her writing, the rights of a divorced woman being almost negligible at that time. In this he failed to recognise the mettle of his opponent, and he lost both the case and the custody of the children. With this success and her subsequent politicking, she did more than any woman before, and few since, to obtain increased rights for her sex.

She was deservedly as much admired by some as she was disapproved of by others, and became the scarcely disguised heroine of George Meredith's novel Diana of the Crossways. *In 1877, at the age of 69, she died only a short*

28

while after she entered her second marriage to an old
friend, Sir William Stirling-Maxwell.

I do not love thee!–no! I do not love thee!
  And yet when thou art absent I am sad;
And envy even the bright blue sky above thee,
  Whose quiet stars may see thee and be glad.

I do not love thee!—yet, I know not why,
  Whate'er thou dost seems still well done, to me:
And often in my solitude I sigh
  That those I do love are not more like thee!

I do not love thee!—yet, when thou art gone,
  I hate the sound (though those who speak be dear)
Which breaks the lingering echo of the tone
  Thy voice of music leaves upon my ear.

I do not love thee!—yet thy speaking eyes,
  With their deep, bright, and most expressive
  blue,
Between me and the midnight heaven arise,
  Oftener than any eyes I ever knew.

I know I do not love thee! yet, alas!
  Others will scarcely trust my candid heart:
And oft I catch them smiling as they pass,
  Because they see me gazing where thou art.

OZYMANDIAS
PERCY BYSSHE SHELLEY

I met a traveller from an antique land,
Who said: Two vast and trunkless legs of stone
Stand in the desert. Near them on the sand,
Half sunk, a shattered visage lies, whose frown
And wrinkled lip and sneer of cold command
Tell that its sculptor well those passions read,
Which yet survive stamped on these lifeless things,
The hand that mocked them and the heart that fed:
And on the pedestal these words appear:
'My name is Ozymandias, King of Kings:
Look on my works, ye Mighty, and despair!'
Nothing beside remains. Round the decay
Of that colossal wreck, boundless and bare
The lone and level sands stretch far away.

Born in 1770 and brought up in Cumbria, he went to St John's College in Cambridge, but left as he turned twenty to walk in Europe. He loved France, held a naïve belief in the justice of the French Revolution, and had a daughter by Annette Vallon, with whom he fell passionately in love. Back in England, like many poets, money was often a worry, and these worries were shared, as they still are, by being among other writers. A close friendship with Coleridge ended with an argument, and just before he was thirty he ended up back in the Lake District sharing a cottage with his sister, Dorothy. Three years later they both went to France to visit Annette Vallon, and soon after that he married Mary Hutchinson, with whom he had been at school in Penrith. He was not well treated by his fellow poets, who were critical. Browning Shelley and Byron all dismissed him as dull. Even Keats, whom he praised, was grudging in return.

Yet his output, and his life, tend to show that he was far from dull. He travelled, he gave love whole-heartedly, he worked stupendously, and he is an interesting man to learn more about. Perhaps you can start with the love letters between him and his wife Mary. Nor should you ignore the writings of his sister Dorothy.

I wander'd lonely as a cloud
    That floats on high o'er vales and hills,
When all at once I saw a crowd,
    A host, of golden daffodils;
Beside the lake, beneath the trees,
Fluttering and dancing in the breeze.

Continuous as the stars that shine
    And twinkle on the Milky Way,
They stretch'd in never-ending line
    Along the margin of a bay:
Ten thousand saw I at a glance,
Tossing their heads in sprightly dance.

The waves beside them danced, but they
    Outdid the sparkling waves in glee:
A poet could not but be gay,
    In such a jocund company:
I gazed—and gazed—but little thought
What wealth the show to me had brought.

For oft, when on my couch I lie
    In vacant or in pensive mood,
They flash upon that inward eye
    Which is the bliss of solitude;
And then my heart with pleasure fills,
And dances with the daffodils.

It was a Lover and his Lass,
   With a hey, and a ho, and a hey nonino,
That o'er the green corn-field did pass,
   In the spring time, the only pretty ring time,
When birds do sing, hey ding a ding, ding;
Sweet lovers love the spring.

Between the acres of the rye,
   With a hey, and a ho, and a hey nonino,
These pretty country folk would lie,
   In the spring time, the only pretty ring time,
When the birds do sing, hey ding a ding, ding;
Sweet lovers love the spring.

This carol they began that hour,
   With a hey, and a ho, and a hey nonino,
How that life was but a flower
   In the spring time, the only pretty ring time,
When the birds do sing, hey ding a ding, ding;
Sweet lovers love the spring.

And, therefore, take the present time
   With a hey, and a ho, and a hey nonino,
For love is crownèd with the prime
   In the spring time, the only pretty ring time,
When the birds do sing, hey ding a ding, ding;
Sweet lovers love the spring.

Let me not to the marriage of true minds
Admit impediments. Love is not love
Which alters when it alteration finds,
Or bends with the remover to remove:
O, no! it is an ever-fixèd mark,
That looks on tempests and is never shaken;
It is the star to every wand'ring bark,
Whose worth's unknown, although his height be
    taken.
Love's not Time's fool, though rosy lips and cheeks
Within his bending sickle's compass come;
Love alters not with his brief hours and weeks,
But bears it out even to the edge of doom:—
    If this be error and upon me proved,
    I never writ, nor no man ever loved.

My heart leaps up when I behold
   A rainbow in the sky:
So was it when my life began;
So is it now I am a man;
So be it when I shall grow old,
   Or let me die!
The Child is father of the Man;
And I could wish my days to be
Bound each to each by natural piety.

SIR PHILIP SIDNEY (1554-1586)

This man was one of nature's heroes. They are thrown up every once in a while, full of promise but dying young, like Raymond Asquith (whose letters you should read) who was killed in the 14-18 War.

Every father wanted him to marry his daughter. He was a soldier, a statesman, a diplomat, a writer, a patron and yet it was only at the age of 31 that he was knighted and was given the political appointments that everyone expected he would have been given years before.

The following year he died of a wound received attacking a Spanish arms train in Holland, where he was Governor of Flushing.

It is said that he gave his water bottle to another wounded man, saying that he needed it less than the other.

My true love hath my heart, and I have his,
    By just exchange for one another given:
I hold his dear, and mine he cannot miss,
    There was never a better bargain driven:
        My true love hath my heart, and I have his.

His heart in me keeps him and me in one,
    My heart in him his thoughts and senses guides:
He loves my heart for once it was his own,
    I cherish his because in me it bides:
        My true love hath my heart, and I have his.

THE BURIAL OF SIR JOHN MOORE
AFTER CORUNNA
CHARLES WOLFE (1791-1823)

Wolfe died at the age of 31 in 1823. He was curate of Donaughnore in County Down for the last three years of his twenties. This poem was published in the Newry Register in 1817, and is probably the only one he wrote that will ever be remembered.

Not a drum was heard, not a funeral note,
    As his corse to the rampart we hurried;
Not a soldier discharged his farewell shot
    O'er the grave where our hero we buried.

We buried him darkly at dead of night,
    The sods with our bayonets turning,
By the struggling moonbeam's misty light
    And the lanthorn dimly burning.

No useless coffin enclosed his breast,
    Not in sheet or in shroud we wound him;
But he lay like a warrior taking his rest
    With his martial cloak around him.

Few and short were the prayers we said,
    And we spoke not a word of sorrow;
But we steadfastly gazed on the face that was dead,
And we bitterly thought of the morrow.

We thought, as we hollow'd his narrow bed
    And smooth'd down his lonely pillow,
That the foe and the stranger would tread o'er his
        head,
    And we far away walk on the billow!

Lightly they'll talk of the spirit that's gone,
    And o'er his cold ashes upbraid him—
But little he'll reck, if they let him sleep on
    In the grave where a Briton has laid him.

But half of our heavy task was done
    When the clock struck the hour for retiring;
And we heard the distant and random gun
    That the foe was sullenly firing.

Slowly and sadly we laid him down,
    From the field of his fame fresh and gory;
We carved not a line, and we raised not a stone,
    But we left him alone with his glory.

Now sleeps the crimson petal, now the white;
Nor waves the cypress in the palace walk;
Nor winks the gold fin in the porphyry font:
The firefly wakens: waken thou with me.

Now droops the milk-white peacock like a ghost,
And like a ghost she glimmers on to me.

Now lies the Earth all Danaë to the stars,
And all thy heart lies open unto me.

Now slides the silent meteor on, and leaves
A shining furrow, as thy thoughts in me.

Now folds the lily all her sweetness up,
And slips into the bosom of the lake:
So fold thyself, my dearest, thou, and slip
Into my bosom and be lost in me.

O Wild West Wind, thou breath of Autumn's
    being,
  Thou from whose unseen presence the leaves
    dead
Are driven like ghosts from an enchanter fleeing,

  Yellow, and black, and pale, and hectic red,
  Pestilence-stricken multitudes! O thou
  Who chariotest to their dark wintery bed

The wingèd seeds, where they lie cold and low,
  Each like a corpse within its grave, until
Thine azure sister of the Spring shall blow

  Her clarion o'er the dreaming earth, and fill
(Driving sweet buds like flocks to feed in air)
  With living hues and odours plain and hill;

Wild Spirit, which art moving everywhere;
Destroyer and preserver; hear, O hear!

SONNET NUMBER 18
WILLIAM SHAKESPEARE

Shall I compare thee to a Summer's day?
Thou art more lovely and more temperate:
Rough winds do shake the darling buds of May,
And Summer's lease hath all too short a date:
Sometime too hot the eye of heaven shines,
And often is his gold complexion dimm'd;
And every fair from fair sometimes declines,
By chance or nature's changing course untrimm'd:
But thy eternal Summer shall not fade
Nor lose possession of that fair thou owest;
Nor shall Death brag thou wanderest in his shade,
When in eternal lines to time thou growest:
 So long as men can breathe, or eyes can see,
 So long lives this, and this gives life to thee.

LUCY (PART II)

WILLIAM WORDSWORTH

She dwelt among the untrodden ways
  Beside the springs of Dove,
A Maid whom there were none to praise
  And very few to love:

A violet by a mossy stone
  Half hidden from the eye!
Fair as a star, when only one
  Is shining in the sky.

She lived unknown, and few could know
  When Lucy ceased to be;
But she is in her grave, and oh,
  The difference to me!

ITYLUS
ALGERNON CHARLES SWINBURNE
(1837-1909)

Swinburne was a promiscuous writer in both senses of the word. A large part of his output was in verse drama, but it was his verse and his pre-occupation with sado-masochism which brought him abuse from some people and what was, and still is to some extent, near veneration from others. Just as the poems of Donne have shaped the literary landscape for many young women, so have Swinburne's poems done the same for many young men.

By the time he had turned forty he was in danger of succumbing to excesses both sexual and alcoholic. But he was saved by a solicitor turned litterateur called Theodore Watts-Dunton, who in 1879 took him to live in Putney for the remaining thirty years of his life.

Swallow, my sister, O sister swallow,
How can thine heart be full of the spring?
A thousand summers are over and dead.
What hast thou found in the spring to follow?
What hast thou found in thine heart to sing?
What wilt thou do when the summer is shed?

O swallow, sister, O fair swift swallow,
Why wilt thou fly after spring to the south,
The soft south whither thine heart is set?
Shall not the grief of the old time follow?
Shall not the song thereof cleave to thy mouth?
Hast thou forgotten ere I forget?

Sister, my sister, O fleet sweet swallow,
  Thy way is long to the sun and the south;
    But I, fulfill'd of my heart's desire,
Shedding my song upon height, upon hollow,
  From tawny body and sweet small mouth
    Feed the heart of the night with fire.

I the nightingale all spring through,
  O swallow, sister, O changing swallow,
    All spring through till the spring be done,
Clothed with the light of the night on the dew,
  Sing, while the hours and the wild birds follow,
    Take flight and follow and find the sun.

Sister, my sister, O soft light swallow,
  Though all things feast in the spring's guest
      chamber,
    How hast thou heart to be glad thereof yet?
For where thou fliest I shall not follow,
  Till life forget and death remember,
    Till thou remember and I forget.

Swallow, my sister, O singing swallow,
  I know not how thou hast heart to sing.
    Hast thou the heart? is it all past over?
Thy lord the summer is good to follow,
  And fair the feet of thy lover the spring:
    But what wilt thou say to the spring thy
        lover?

O swallow, sister, O fleeting swallow,
  My heart in me is a molten ember
    And over my head the waves have met.

But thou wouldst tarry or I would follow
    Could I forget or thou remember,
        Couldst thou remember and I forget.

O sweet stray sister, O shifting swallow,
    The heart's division divideth us.
        Thy heart is light as a leaf of a tree;
But mine goes forth among sea-gulfs hollow
    To the place of the slaying of Itylus,
        The feast of Daulis, the Thracian sea.

O swallow, sister, O rapid swallow,
    I pray thee sing not a little space.
        Are not the roofs and the lintels wet?
The woven web that was plain to follow,
    The small slain body, the flower-like face,
        Can I remember if thou forget?

O sister, sister, thy first-begotten!
    The hands that cling and the feet that follow,
        The voice of the child's blood crying yet,
Who hath remember'd me? who hath forgotten?
    Thou hast forgotten, O summer swallow,
        But the world shall end when I forget.

Take, O take those lips away,
   That so sweetly were forsworn;
And those eyes, the break of day,
   Lights that do mislead the morn!
But my kisses bring again,
      Bring again;
Seals of love, but seal'd in vain,
      Seal'd in vain!

Tell me where is Fancy bred,
    Or in the heart or in the head?
How begot, how nourishèd?
        Reply, reply.
It is engender'd in the eyes,
With gazing fed; and Fancy dies
In the cradle where it lies.
    Let us all ring Fancy's knell:
    I'll begin it,—Ding, dong, bell.
All: Ding, dong, bell.

FROM 'AS YOU LIKE IT'
WILLIAM SHAKESPEARE

Under the greenwood tree,
Who loves to lie with me,
And turn his merry note
Unto the sweet bird's throat,
Come hither, come hither, come hither:
        Here shall he see
        No enemy
But winter and rough weather.

    Who doth ambition shun,
And loves to live i' the sun,
Seeking the food he eats,
    And pleased with what he gets,
Come hither, come hither, come hither:
        Here shall he see
        No enemy
But winter and rough weather.

Jacques replies:
    If it do come to pass
    That any man turn ass,
    Leaving his wealth and ease
    A stubborn will to please,
Ducdamè, ducdamè, ducdamè:
        Here shall he see
            Gross fools as he,
An if he will come to me.

ARTHUR WILLIAM EDGAR
O'SHAUGHNESSY (1844-1881)

Longevity seems to be the lot of conductors. It is not a lot
shared by many poets. O'Shaughnessy in his short life
worked in the British Museum Library, was friends with
the pre-Raphaelites, was the author of several books of
poetry, and died at the age of thirty seven.

We are the music-makers,
   And we are the dreamers of dreams,
Wandering by lone sea-breakers,
And sitting by desolate streams;
World-losers and world-forsakers,
   On whom the pale moon gleams:
Yet we are the movers and shakers
   Of the world for ever, it seems.

With wonderful deathless ditties
We build up the world's great cities,
   And out of a fabulous story
   We fashion an empire's glory:
One man with a dream, at pleasure,
   Shall go forth and conquer a crown;
And thee with a new song's measure
   Can trample an empire down.

We, in the ages lying
   In the buried past of the earth,
Built Nineveh with our sighing,

And Babel itself with our mirth;
And o'erthrew them with prophesying
    To the old of the new world's worth;
For each age is a dream that is dying,
    Or one that is coming to birth.

Wilfred Owen was almost accidentally a poet. The son of a stationmaster in Shropshire he was from an early age immersed in books. And, like many like-minded young men at that time, he wrote verse. In 1913, at the age of twenty he went to teach English in Bordeaux. It was not until 1915, when it was clear that the Great War was not the short war that had been expected, that he returned to Britain and joined the army.

Concussed and ill after a tour in France he was sent to Dr Rivers' hospital in Edinburgh, where he met Siegfried Sassoon, who was also a patient. Sassoon was embarrassing the establishment by protesting against the War both publicly and by means of his uncompromising poetry, too harsh and unromantic for many tastes. But since he was a holder of the MC, of which he eventually became ashamed, he could not be called a coward.

To see the thought in the annotations that Sassoon made or suggested to Wilfrid Owen's poetry it is not unreasonable to think that, had it not been both for the War and this chance meeting, we would never have heard of Owen again. It was Sassoon, too, who did so much to get Owen's poems into print. Only five were published while he was alive.

Time has shown his writing to be among the very best of all war poetry, and if we find it sad that he was killed in the last week of the war, having also received his own MC, we have to be grateful that he survived long enough to leave us what he did. This poem is probably his best known, and albeit somewhat more corny than many of the others, it was exactly right for the message at that time.

What passing-bells for these who die as cattle?
    Only the monstrous anger of the guns.
    Only the stuttering rifles' rapid rattle
Can patter out their hasty orisons.

No mockeries for them from prayers or bells,
    Nor any voice of mourning save the choirs,—
The shrill, demented choirs of wailing shells;
    And bugles calling for them from sad shires.

What candles many be held to speed them all?
    Not in the hands of boys, but in their eyes
Shall shine the holy glimmers of good-byes.
    The pallor of girls' brows shall be their pall;
Their flowers the tenderness of silent minds,
And each slow dusk a drawing-down of blinds.

There are more people who acknowledge that Wagner was a great composer than enjoy his operas. It must also be true that there are more people who acknowledge that Milton was a great poet than enjoy his poetry.

Wordsworth was not one of them, for it was he who wrote the sonnet that begins 'Milton, thou should be living at this hour: England hath need of thee: she is a fen of stagnant waters:'

It is possible that Paradise Lost *and* Paradise Regained *were more read in the days when there were fewer alternative attractions for an evening's entertainment.*

Crossword compilers would expect people to have been obliged to read these poems, and probably to learn parts of L'Allegro, Il Penseroso *and* Lycidas, *but even these are too long to be afforded a space in this little book.*

Some of us do not warm to him as Wordsworth did.

On the one hand he published the view (justification perhaps?) that those who were not chaste before marriage were more likely to be constant after it. On the other he was as puritanical and unforgiving as any of the Cromwellians of his time. He appears to have treated his children with repellent harshness. Yet there are his contemporaries who assure us that he was warm-hearted and kindly.

There is enough in print about Milton to give you a chance to form your own views.

When I consider how my light is spent,
  E're half my days, in this dark world and wide,
  And that one Talent which is death to hide,
  Lodg'd with me useless, though my Soul more
    bent,
To serve therewith my Maker, and present
  My true account, least He returning chide,
  'Doth God exact day-labour, light deny'd?'
  I fondly ask: But patience to prevent
That murmur, soon replies, 'God doth not need
  Either man's work or his own gifts. Who best
  Bear his milde yoak, they serve him best. His
    State
Is Kingly: thousands at his bidding speed
  And post o're Land and Ocean without rest;
  They also serve who only stand and wait.'

When in the chronicle of wasted time
I see descriptions of the fairest wights,
And beauty making beautiful old rime
In praise of Ladies dead and lovely Knights;
Then, in the blazon of sweet beauty's best,
Of hand, of foot, of lip, of eye, of brow,
I see their antique pen would have exprest
Even such a beauty as you master now.
So all their praises are but prophecies
Of this our time, all you prefiguring;
And for they look'd but with divining eyes,
They had not skill enough your worth to sing:
    For we, which now behold these present days,
    Have eyes to wonder, but lack tongues to praise.

wight = man

CHORUS FROM 'ATALANTA'
ALGERNON CHARLES SWINBURNE

When the hounds of spring are on winter's traces,
    The mother of months in meadow or plain
Fills the shadows and windy places
    With lisp of leaves and ripple of rain;
And the brown bright nightingale amorous
Is half assuaged for Itylus,
For the Thracian ships and the foreign faces,
    The tongueless vigil, and all the pain.

Come with bows bent and with emptying of quivers,
    Maiden most perfect, lady of light,
With a noise of winds and many rivers,
    With a clamour of waters, and with might;
Bind on thy sandals, O thou most fleet,
Over the splendour and speed of thy feet;
For the faint east quickens, the wan west shivers,
    Round the feet of the day and the feet of the night.

Where shall we find her, how shall we sing to her,
    Fold our hands round her knees, and cling?
O that man's heart were as fire and could spring to her,
    Fire, or the strength of the streams that spring!
For the stars and the winds are unto her
As raiment, as songs of the harp-player;
For the risen stars and the fallen cling to her,
    And the southwest-wind and the west-wind sing.
For winter's rains and ruins are over,
    And all the season of snows and sins;

The days dividing lover and lover,
    The light that loses, the night that wins;
And time remember'd is grief forgotten,
And frosts are slain and flowers begotten,
And in green underwood and cover
    Blossom by blossom the spring begins.

The full streams feed on flower of rushes,
    Ripe grasses trammel a travelling foot,
The faint fresh flame of the young year flushes
    From leaf to flower and flower to fruit;
And fruit and leaf are as gold and fire,
And the oat is heard above the lyre,
And the hoofèd heel of a satyr crushes
    The chestnut-husk at the chestnut-root.

And Pan by noon and Bacchus by night,
    Fleeter of foot that the fleet-foot kid,
Follows with dancing and fills with delight
    The Mænad and the Bassarid;
And soft as lips that laugh and hide
The laughing leaves of the trees divide,
And screen from seeing and leave in sight
    The god pursuing, the maiden hid.

The ivy falls with the Bacchanal's hair
    Over her eyebrows hiding her eyes;
The wild vine slipping down leaves bare
    Her bright breast shortening into sighs;
The wild vine slips with the weight of its leaves,
But the berried ivy catches and cleaves
To the limbs that glitter, the feet that scare
    The wolf that follows, the fawn that flies.

Where the bee sucks, there suck I
In a cowslip's bell I lie;
There I couch when owls do cry.
On the bat's back I do fly
After summer merrily:
    Merrily, merrily, shall I live now,
    Under the blossom that hangs on the bough.

Where the remote Bermudas ride
In the ocean's bosom unespied,
From a small boat that row'd along
The listening winds received this song:
   'What should we do but sing His praise
that led us through the watery maze
unto an isle so long unknown,
and yet far kinder than our own?
Where He the huge sea-monsters wracks,
That lift the deep upon their backs,
He lands us on a grassy stage,
Safe from the storms' and prelates' rage;
He gave us this eternal Spring
Which here enamels everything,
And sends the fowls to us in care
On daily visits through the air:
He hangs in shades the orange bright
Like golden lamps in a green night,
And does in the pomegranates close
Jewels more rich that Ormus shows:
He makes the figs our mouths to meet
And throws the melons at our feet;
But apples plants of such a price,
No tree could ever bear them twice.
With cedars chosen by His hand
From Lebanon He stores the land;
And makes the hollow seas that roar
Proclaim the ambergris on shore.

He cast (of which we rather boast)
The Gospel's pearl upon our coast;
And in these rocks for us did frame
A temple where to sound His name.
O, let our voice His praise exalt
Till it arrive at Heaven's vault,
Which thence (perhaps) rebounding may
Echo beyond the Mexique bay!'

Thus sung they in the English boat
A holy and a cheerful note:
And all the way, to guide their chime,
With falling oars they kept the time.

Who is Silvia? What is she?
    That all our swains commend her?
Holy, fair, and wise is she;
    The heavens such grace did lend her,
That she might admirèd be.

Is she kind as she is fair?
    For beauty lives with kindness:
Love doth to her eyes repair,
    To help him of his blindness;
And, being help'd, inhabits there.

Then to Silvia let us sing,
    That Silvia is excelling;
She excels each mortal thing
Upon the dull earth dwelling:
To her let us garlands bring.

Another of the 'Tribe of Ben', Suckling was born with every advantage – brains, money and charm. He travelled widely, was knighted for his diplomatic skills, and lived luxuriously at the court of Charles the First. But before he was thirty four he was dead, said to have committed suicide in Paris. Sad.
Another of his poems begins

> 'Out upon it, I have loved,
> Three whole days together;
> And am like to love three more,
> If it prove fair weather.'

A better read than old Milton.

Why so pale and wan, fond lover?
Prithee, why so pale?
Will, when looking well can't move her,
   Looking ill prevail?
   Prithee, why so pale?

Why so dull and mute, young sinner?
   Prithee, why so mute?
Will, when speaking well can't win her,
   Saying nothing do't?
   Prithee, why so mute?

Quit, quit for shame! This will not move;
   This cannot take her.
If of herself she will not love,
   Nothing can make her:
   The devil take her!

Wotton was another too now inconsidered star in that constellation that flourished at the end of the 16th and the beginning of the 17th centuries.

After Oxford he entered the Middle Temple. He was then used by the Earl of Essex to gather intelligence abroad. For twenty years until 1624 he was a diplomat and Izaak Walton in his biography of Wotton tells us he originated the definition of an ambassador as 'an honest man sent to lie abroad for the good of his country'.

He was provost of Eton. He wrote about architecture. He published other writing. And he wrote poems like this.

You meaner beauties of the night,
    That poorly satisfy our eyes
More by your number than your light,
    You common people of the skies;
    What are you when the moon shall rise?

You curious chanters of the wood,
    That warble forth Dame Nature's lays,
Thinking your passions understood
    By your weak accents; what's your praise
    When Philomel her voice shall raise?

You violets that first appear,
    By your pure purple mantles known
Like the proud virgins of the year,
    As if the spring were all your own;
    What are you when the rose is blown?

63

So, when my mistress shall be seen
   In form and beauty of her mind,
By virtue first, then choice, a Queen,
   Tell me, if she were not design'd
   Th' eclipse and glory of her kind.